Its Halting Measure

Other publications by John Welch include:

The Fish God Problem (The Many Press, London 1977)
And Ada Ann, A Book of Narratives
                    (Great Works Press, Bishops Stortford 1978)
Out Walking (Anvil, London 1984)
Blood and Dreams (Reality Street Editions, London 1991)
Its Radiance (Poetical Histories, Cambridge 1993)
Greeting Want (infernal methods, Cambridge 1997)
The Eastern Boroughs (Shearsman Books, Exeter 2004)
On Orkney (infernal methods, Stromness 2005)
Collected Poems (Shearsman Books, Exeter, 2008)
Visiting Exile (Shearsman Books, Exeter, 2009)

Prose
Dreaming Arrival (Shearsman Books, Exeter, 2008)

As editor:
Stories from South Asia (Oxford University Press, 1984)

Its Halting Measure

John Welch

Shearsman Books

First published in the United Kingdom in 2012 by
Shearsman Books
50 Westons Hill Drive
Emersons Green
Bristol
BS16 7DF

http://www.shearsman.com/

ISBN 978-1-84861-243-3

Acknowledgements
Some of these poems previously appeared in the following
print and online magazines:

*Blackbox Manifold, The Bowwow Shop, Fire, The Fortnightly Review,
fragmente, The Interpreter's House, Litter, Meridian, Navis,
nthposition, Object Permanence, Palantir, The Reader,
Tears in the Fence, Tenth Muse, Terrible Work*

'Entering the Light' was published in
Plant Care: Poems for Mimi Khalvati

Contents

4: The Baffler

one: voice in a mirror

Printing: the art of turning paper into emotions

Is printed, in ink that won't come off on your hands
Writing that blackened the mirror searching for change,

In winter sunshine the dustless afternoon clouds,
The voice-performer's light-filled skeleton.

John Sell Cotman: 'Trees in the Alban Hills'

Some force, in among them, a
Driving apart
Where the wind gets in there all among those trees
Perched on a hillside, over against the city
As if the god were there,
A sort of visionary absence?

Four Walks

Floating Cargo
Cheshunt to Broxbourne and back

Walking steadily
Like this beside the water
Does bring a certain kind of peace.
Discarded blossom lies along the surface,
All this stuff that's drifting down
And a powerful scent of elder
Whose musk is edged with sweetness.
People you pass are not quite sure
Whether or not to greet you
And here's a sort of bollard,
It's like an abandoned phallus.
Trees have that hint of greyness—
Sunlit upturned leaf drama
Against a dark threat of sky.
You carry on, through surprising groves
Putting some distance under your feet
Till, breaking into the open
Space of a silent field, there are
Unmoving clouds
And what's this shrub with whitish flowers,
Its musty-spermy smell?
You turn back to that waterside
Whose floating cargo of blossom
Is almost as motionless as text.

Near Guiting Power

Used as title, a taking possession,
It does have this 'watch-me-doing-this' aspect
Like a man with that falsely knowing expression
Who, looking self-consciously relaxed,
Has briefly rediscovered the joys of reading.
But the hedgerow flail has been this way
Leaving twigs like the chopped ends of thumbs
And a bird in the mist is making a gargling sound.
Things unseen beckon, as we move on
Heads down into the wind. The Cotswolds?
It's well-behaved children, on well-behaved horses.
It's probably the English Tuscany,
Wealth carefully hidden behind the trees
Like that Roman villa in Spoonley Wood
Gone now to a heap of stones.
The villa is real enough, the mosaic
A Victorian fake, under an old tarpaulin.
Out in the open again,
The furtive sound of an unseen plane.
It's the details that still have the power
To make you happy—that cotoneaster
Flaring out over a wall, red berries
And dense, bare, almost feathery twigs,
Solitary trees, stock still
As if they were the substance of our thought.

London Loop
Bexley to Petts Wood

thin covering of cloud
excitement of starting out

skylarks and doggerel   traffic
tipping this way, it empties itself for you –

a landfill site?
continuous traffic's a curtain now, useless angers

. . .

a sort of special thing
for throwing a ball for it

five arches bridge
a 'visual climax'

a semblance of gratitude
to free up what's inside you

here's a monster celtic cross
'the founder of cable and wireless'

she tells me and
'fourteen lead-lined coffins –

we have many important people here
from the big houses'

well, everyone's marginal
shavings of birdsong   a central process

. . .

a stagnant pond in a wood
and a viewing platform

discarded beer cans
someone has torched the 'kissing gate'

puzzling pastoral remnant
what people come to these hidden places to do

alcohol   fire   as offerings
in the hot twinkling wood

anemones and others
each individual flower very pure

Deal to Dover

The cloud-heart melts away
Lord de Tabley

So, the surprise   of nothing being found
the pupil shrinks in so much light

and our restlessness, against
an odd still sea
its peculiar deeps and blues—

Danger Of Death
No Diving
No Jumping
            the sea's
steep syllables.

When the reader gets up from the book
it is as if almost in paradise
and still there is that expanse before him.
Imagining it an audience
and it saying 'I want every inch of you'
but he has no name to find it with.

    Mid-afternoon, yes
  but why should words help,
  what *is* beyond
  this beckoning?

            It had
fixed itself
like a brooch
but awkwardly, at his side.

and how the night becomes us
when you'll fit me like a glove,
you and I
meticulous graveyard of speech.

Two Landscapes / Garden Escapes

1

Cybele headless
on the Palatine
in front of her the thick, soft dust
whose footprints in it?
A bunch of mimosa someone left
has faded in her lap.

Mother of a Roman afternoon
of traffic.   The city was
a slow paste, grey and ochre

The dark and dusty green of pines

scent of Cybele such an other absence
such
as music lifts   one
inch above   no
more

The lopped head   like a monstrous absence
a blatant thing devoid of eyes

2
Wind wrestled nylon around you
where a gull went over
spoiled landscape of garage and gravel pit
I too can be on the earth

he said, I want
some of that
being alone: just
there!

Mud, water, a grey but marching sky
a tremendous rawness
miscellaneous bushes
garden escapes I shouldn't wonder.

Imagine, that
messed-up landscape, it corresponds to me
and its single gull flies over,
the would-be transcendental
veering home in the wind
all that muscle against the air its home

The Return

No change in the town
But dumb noise in its
Saturday streets.

Its people reside
Among stone, and
Traffic as always

Drifts in exuberant
Stasis. The doom
Now or never

Takes hold
As the houses come
Down, and are scattered

By slow heavy winds.
Places become new places,
The same knot being woven and woven

And birds veering off
Being launched from ramparts
At an approach of feet,

Like exiles, the towers and
Shafts of sun, fabrications
That glint in its shining.

...

The grove at
Midday, heat
Flies in and out
Among the iron
Trunks, there is
A din of insects
From the interior.

A message of wind
Now tops the hill,
Below, ideas
For red brick havens.
Bushes lean into
The hill's side
Where whitish bloom
Gives off its musky odour.

Here we have come
With our harsh boxed music
Among swelling chestnuts.
Arriving with cameras
We have brought wrapped food
And cups, to the
Fringe of the grove
And our games. I
Like this nearness,
Cramped festivity.
Roots seek the dark,
And hunt around –
Launch flowers from dust.

What I would miss
At all times is
These streets whose air is
Dulled with ghosts,
The one who keeps
A bar, her face
A squashed rose launched
From nowhere, now
Official birds
That rise in clouds
To name the sky.

...

Now sparrows roost among yellowing
Sycamore leaves by the market.

Where a faithless sun declines there are
Hundreds of the shrill balls of feathers.

Only one half of a person I'm here
My lips moving soundlessly to my tread.

At the front door I look for my key
Stand on the moment's threshold and listen—
The buzzing of the codes.

So it goes to an abstract colour
But urgent at the margin.
Riding along the rim –
And looking out over the waterworks
Yellow sky breathed a word

So my mind went
With the bird up there
Always   away
Then winter coming on like this,
Passing the house again and looking
Up at the lit silence
Of what was once your flat
And we were falling
Further and further back, towards
The sheet of glass that lifted
Its gleaming blackness sheer against
A night of restless unseen trees.

And a face, growing dark with the recognising
Of what it was between us—
Why is it called 'making' love
As if in the mirror it
Looked and saw difference, out of the
All but unreachable depths
Elbowing reflections aside?

Surely we were on our way to somewhere,
If we only knew
But I was flying with the wish
To empty 'me' into 'you'
And later all it wanted was
To be indoors and quiet,
Inhabiting a morning.

The words had put me in a shallow grave,
Holding you holding me and falling
Further and further back, and now
At memory's far edge, still falling
Towards the blackness of that silent
Window one more time.

...

Opus Posthumous

Crashing around inside his wintry lusts,
The brake, the grove, the riverbank—
It overflows with fitful February.

The tombs, the tombs are overgrown.

Our pub is called The Albion
Return Return.
It sheltered us from a May storm.
If the laurel fits you wear it.

Little children trapped in school
Parrot the names.

The Carpet

At 5 o'clock heat
sits in the sky   a brassy shimmer.
By half past ten it's almost dark
slight smears of cloud
over the park. The heat will stay

& night is only
a lifting away from this.
I move in the spread of air

an appetite that
looks for rest.

...

It was in the night
I had no time
but crept out in the dark

last thing at night and there was
breeze everywhere in the leaves

a musty intriguing odour where
the elder-tree bending down
succeeded to the ripe scent of the iris.

Being pressed against my singleness—
the invisible pane of the air
first there was
nothing, then there were children.

Moving in you I'm nowhere
this night-breeze touching
the inside of a thigh.

…

It hides itself it hides itself in sweetness.
Here I am in the thickness of my cloud
and the large moon-pale of you –
I have lost what you have found.

In here the carpet's pattern simply waits
like a fall of stained glass
blunting my tread, the close wool.

…

It is for you I'll
cross the city
mere shadow of myself
through gritty dawn-wind streets.

Dawn-chorus walk
the ruined cemetery
its bible of leaf-light where sun slants.
The rose window has no glass.

The dark mongrel pigeons match the stone
restlessly swarm round the frame.
Flying in and out
they tumble over each other.

Your threshold's where the
light bends down
and bare boards of that room
are my waiting to be made.

And your embrace is my being seen
in tender colour.
Footprint of light
I am insistent at your door.

...

Swift flew in through my workroom window.
I found it early one morning.
It was crawling up the red cloth

that odd blunt head
quick circling eyes.
It was like the little bit
left over from a dream.

I shook it out of the cloth.
It collapsed in its heap of wings.

You came in, in your nightdress.
Cupping your hands you held it
then you threw this thing at the sky!

My scissor-winged visitor
sailing and circling away.
A piece of the sooty colour
he has nothing to own but the sky.

I had not seen anything
more perfectly adapted
and compared to this
I am a clumsy accident.
Holding a piece of the sky
it was given then taken back, being
briefly held.

The Operation

The calm delirium of consciousness
Adrian Stokes

Six months on and another brain scan.
Mine's almost the first appointment of the day.
I walked there from the Angel through morning mist,
Got briefly lost in the hospital basement's corridors.
Lying inside the machine, told to lie still
Hearing the operator's distorted voice
And that odd grinding booming sound—
It's like being inside a noisy coffin.
I balance my head on its stalk, remember
The operation's aftermath,
Night after night of forcing myself awake.
Was I still fighting the anaesthetic?
I'd make tea, sit in my room upstairs
Helplessly waiting for daylight
And now there's this voice, this thing as odd as a mirror
Telling me 'You are still here',
It sleeps like an animal, wakes me, this something
That has the world in its eye.
With a kind of mad innocence
It follows me round, like someone saying
'It can all be yours,
And you are the fragment in all this
That sets the other fragments flying.'
I'm not sure how it gets me from there to here.
Later, released into air and traffic
I approach the Museum,
Reach in past its strict façade
To a place where everything's made still. In here

My watching's coupled with a wish to touch
This tilted figure taken from a temple,
Arms thrown back, unstoppable
In a sculpted swirl of garments. Holding still
I'm here as if for ever
Watching her resume her headless flying.

Meditate

Space under chest a seed of growth
Mind crosses the paper—

Ink-trace, the flying white—
Sleeps briefly, to wake on the minute.

Cross-legged on the fire cushion,
Active in watchful sitting

Mind so close to itself
So close it lies

On its way to those bones
Buried in a distant range.

Entering the Light

Waking, just before daybreak—
Yes I can be here as well

In the undividedness of birdsong
Waiting on an edge of light.

Now ageing limbs exchange a greeting
Doing small amounts of good in the world

And here it comes again,
The windows in light array

And the human stench forgiven.
This is surely the place

I suffered lyric damage.
As if I could heal it with words

One moment of enough
Might be named as the place where I am

And I thought I might take it home with me,
The undamaged voice of a child.

two: his case

The voice whose stairs he climbs, to begin it all over again. The 'I' that speaks him—what does it want of him? Brain that tricked an I into being, a wide-eyed snatching at self.

A restless uneasy night of enormous dreams and he wonders whether the thing that tears him apart is the thing that makes him. As if he is looking for something that continually empties itself? Out walking first thing next morning he looks up and there it is, a nest's frail perch, and he starts to feel better.

A way, this flying, of hiding up there, bird-man a sort of pause hanging there at the edge of the city, as if about to abandon his sky refuge. Ever the watchful child, he thought he might make a whole book of it, called 'hesitations'.

Flight Reform

1
From the pit between two emerged
This one, an anxious stranger
Now pushing himself toward speech.
A child's in there who still keeps inward house.
He tends the lock

And once, in a dream, he saw him.
He could just make him out, beyond the blurred glass
Late at night coming downstairs.
He was checking the door
Holding his dressing-gown round him,

The boy he was, holding himself together
While all around him the suburb
Dreamed itself away.
He did so try to assemble
The parts of him being crowded in the flesh—

'And if I could find
The distance inside me'.
Something eerily floating, it
Imposes itself, with a dull persistence.
It is so much easier to walk on air.

2

Wounded for survival
He kept the wound fresh, it will
Last till morning in the dream-furrow

To glisten and stir, in that
Grey light-watery place,
Dawn's chorus, while outside

There's last night's shattered windscreen's glass
When houses were so still in streetlamp glare
But how remote that fracture

Daytime makes normal, stepping out
As brisk as this from doorway,
The glass one tidy heap of fragments.

'The places where I left myself
Are what I cannot find,
Well-practised in an art of lying still

And in the act of taking
Flight being always when you'll
See me in my finest plumes

I'll come back with my heap of words
Glinting in the sun.'
The car has gone but they remain.

He Goes Out Walking

1

Hence that man who came into the city.
At a certain moment his flight
Stalled and now, as if with folded wings,
He has something he wants to tell you

Who'd hurried to avoid the light, desk-stranger.
Walking on the side of the road in shadow
He came to waste place dark with sunlight,
Was one who liked the taste ruin made.

'Visiting the place where wings were
Mine was such missionary strangeness
On afternoons where tower blocks
Grow lonely beside water.

In that impossible space
Between object and sign, wing and water
It was my attempt to exist.'
Late over water the accent of a wing . . .

2

Sloping desk-surface
He leaves, returns to

Becoming so aware
Of how far away and on the run he is
To come back as one simple bead of light.
Walking out, out walking
Imagines sealed sunlight-invaded courtyards,

And the sun cautious
At this time of the year
Blindly on the facades of buildings

As, walking through nameless squares
He discovered an absence taller than himself,
'The way this late, low light
Anoints a distant scar
My ruins aired to view.'

3
The shelf, of
Negligible novels
A collection of all the slight lives
And a lunchtime walk to the edge.
Like hearing a

City a long way off
His doorway ended in silence.
In order to make this
He'd lifted the best lines
Raising the latch of silence.

Each 'I' is a nod at the page,
A finger lifted
To the mouth's silent fortress—
The pronoun's where someone drowned,
It still bobs about on the surface.

4

Privet's musk from the towering bush
Of off-white flower, dustings of rain,
Buddleia, lime-flower and petrol smells
And what he is, it
Lifts into itself,
Treads down the morning silence.

'You have been saved from some
Danger and kept for this'.
A war child he can all but remember
The absurd music of that day
When the silence came out of the sky—
'Perhaps it is something I was named for'.

Being here before the rest was made
He was kept safe in a rustle of leaves
And then there was this waking to the world.
As if after a long illness
It collects itself again,
The slippery innocence of 'you'.

Given this ordinary light
All afternoon where it falls on the painting
Now it is how something seen
All by itself can make him happy—
Where she is perched, for instance,
On a concrete seat, an edge of time

While the sound of a plane for-
gets itself in the sky,
And what he imagines—
The canvas being drawn aside,

Is him being taken back, finally
Into the architect's drawing.

His Certain Song

Go Sing It To Her Bones

Infant latched onto its earliest hungers—
Once I was alive, but now I'll sing.
When did my long sleep begin?

Blameless the air I breathe—
As I walked out, into forgiveness of rain
I touched and then forgot to touch my moment.

Today cars bring their bright reflections closer.
Each driver is a ghosted badge.
The park is politics and love

And if I were made
Free of it all in sheer light to imagine
Untainted morning, the blossom descending:

Give me the piece of you I beg.

Wanting Relief From Thought

And will sit here alone—
I want relief from thought.

She came here for me
With her heavy demand

Music, its rub and squeak
Warm rasp of hair

Skin crossed by traffic of sibilants
A perfect twisted road.

To speak from down below there
Where we are, swimming in detail,

Harsh-scented the warm acre.
It will leave me what I can't defend, the

Plain verb talking.

Open Pages

Pages being at rest like wings
Lift their print markings.

A child went down early
Into a dew-soaked garden

But the birds flew up and were gone
So I became bird-watcher

In a garden that fell half into ruin.
Its flowers straggle and stray

And birdsong falls in here like rain.
To be in a garden of full knowing

The birds ascending, de-
scending, substantial ghosts, one dives

Arrow-shaped
Into blossom

As I walk past flowers whose bland faces
Have memorised the sun.

Spill

As the air stirs
On the outermost parts of my
Skin, and what is most
Distant becomes most clear

I am this column, of
Blond light, and the sea here—
Its salt fractions have left their
Slight epidermal

Trace, shallow crystal
As we move to our
Liquid becoming
And I am extended

Outward, yes, grinding air,
Us in the morning together
Shadowed from sunlight
Where the patterned curtain falls

Across. We look back at the flesh.
Ageing but not still
We'll begin to slow
And to spill, like the sea.

The Repair

And the rest of his life? It's as if he were reading
A not very adequate translation
When seeing round the words he thinks he can just make out
The original, where it busies itself
With cooking, sorting papers, arranging flowers.
As he watched one opened like the remains of an eye.

Out walking today on the Heath
The tree harbours a wound.
It glistens and dries where he stands
On a hill and looks at London—
'It was daylight left me here, making signs,
And here are the words that almost found me'.
He'd imagined how they might all come down
In one enormous descending
As the cracked tree's lightning-self
Once held to that split in the light, and standing here
Art gives him the illusion of being.
He is filling the wound with sound.

Gela

Silver didrachm: the coin's obverse shows a naked horseman galloping right, brandishing a spear held high in right hand. On the reverse, fore-part of a man-headed bull, the river god Gelas, swimming right. 490-480 BC.

The part of language that remained abstract,
But he has deciphered himself a plain boy.
That 'father' he sensed at his shoulder
From whom he drank sustenance,
And then that all-mothering margin.
How can he inscribe himself round it
Who'll want to be held after?
'Now give me some fresh words
Here in the cave to quarrel or to be kind.'

...

Death plating a mirror—it tilts,
Dozing and playing the piano, their days
Spending such afternoon wealth.

Whose writing equals a snatching.
Tree standing over water—
Its rooted reflection

Revives him, one withered one red
Berry hung over a blankness of water,
'From such a distance the light falls on me.

Enough of this hiding-being
Among all these unread books,
Nail-clippings and shed hair'.

...

Bull with a man's head,
Minotaur reversed, the
River-swimming god.

'Sung in high air   hung in sighing
Air, let the sky be home, and I
Be grounded here in harsh colour.'

The curve is deathward, ejaculation,
The masculine
An anxiously contrived state,

The small careering rider
Who crosses a bridge of blood,
Engorgement of saying.

Their painted depiction, their writing character
Whose indifference grazes him.
These germinate. They begin.

        …

'As maker of shape I am lonely
And thinking of your small stillness
Should like to sleep kneeling.'

There is warmth where she sleeps,
Her form on the other side of daylight,
Asleep in the house of the enemy

And something wakes up inside him.
Eye blinks at a carnival fresco,
Full moon above the roof. Tree waves by it, he

Stirs. Inwardly
Like a handkerchief tight inside the bud—and
When best to declare its implacable folds?

Print-on-Demand

To have got out from underneath it,
The shadow of all he had written—
Ahead of him each eager hill.

So it is to depart from the page,
As if, getting up from his chair
He stood up in it, breathing the moment
Such was the weight of that silence, lifting
The pile of printed pages—
'I am taken possession of in a different voice'.

'I' lifts
An awkward monument to self—
& what was once all breathing
                                    might quit the air?

three: the hustle alarm

3.3.2 Behavioural factors. Many of the incidents in the database arise not from physical factors, but from behaviour.

From *Minimisation of Accidents at the Platform Train Interface, Halcrow Group Limited in partnership with Human Engineering*

Ambassador

With the ex-ambassador, ninety years old
"I am so well looked after"
Talking Philby and Cairncross,
Darlan, Vichy, de Gaulle,

World events like the fading noise of a city
As I watch the process of my own skin
Alter its landscape, in the slow afternoon
Then return to that small lizard mouth,

His skin on the verge of translucence
Where a sweet-natured man
Is gratefully eating the flesh off the bone.
"I shall permit myself a small whisky."

Leaving next day we met the ambassador,
Green-shirted, waving and calling
"Jane is off shopping somewhere".
He was bright as the insect kingdom

As it dances its moment of being,
Not quite our stilted epiphanies
Here in *la France profonde*
Where death waits with perfect manners.

The ambassador, plenipotentiary
Full of death's powers, who moved
Carefully on two sticks
Still knocking at the door of the world.

Canary Wharf

In an East London classroom a girl told me a story about her father when he first came from Pakistan to London. He looked out of an upstairs window and saw Canary Wharf in the distance. Thinking it was quite near he set out to walk there and came back hours later having got completely lost.

'Historic Limehouse' accessed via
A bafflement of notices
And I imagine him
Wading through these signs
That suddenly infest the landscape
Docklands, our gaze a kind of edge,
And glass towers like a cargo cult
To draw down money.
Watching the way a life
Congeals into possessions,
A sort of half-hearted quest,
Its muted gloss like cooling fat—
But hereabouts there is
An ancient smell of water,
Fish-scales illusion city shimmer
Exiguous catch   this tower.

'In Riots of the Upper Air'
For Fawzi Karim

Your poem, here it halts in English
And they say the language speaks you. So is this a trap?
As for me I seek to stretch out in these spaces
Made by exile's peculiar travel
As if I too spent my life between here and there,
Between the blossom and its fall.

Walking out of the dentist's and into the street
My tongue explores the damage.
I'm stiffer with age walking around in a city.
Can someone tell me the name of the procession
Passing these trees
As if they had just landed on the earth?

Trying to discover the secret of their balance,
A certain silence springs out from each trunk
As somewhere another bomber
Lifts, slow as a statue, away from its plinth of shadow—
Another dictator past his sell-by date,
A government discovering righteousness?

Being shaken with useless rages
We wonder how not to do harm
Like trailing a broken branch.
Here is a bush of white flowers in flattish clusters,
A harsh honeyish smell that I recognise
But cannot name. Unreal the hiss of blossom.

In Camera

Out walking and you pass it
In its lonely trance of watching,
A peculiar kind of witnessing,
Authority shivered into a million forms.

How to distil this presence?

This thing with a crick in its neck
Like someone always looking over his shoulder,
This thing that aims all round itself
Instead of a head has grown

An all-encompassing gaze.

It thinks it sees, it sees, and thinks
When is a person actually a person?
Perhaps it's that young man, his careful stroll
Hooded and watchful through the afternoon?

And now he's all but out of range.

Parkforce! There are frail new trees
And a skyline of antennae.
What difference does it make
To the one who walks through this?

As if through a hall of mirrors?

Chilly receptacle, it never shows its face,
Its surface splits like an insect's faceted eye
Or like a timid bird of prey declares
'Our actions are proportionate'

'We'll get you if you feel like it'

Being made almost entirely of such words:
'Proportionate' 'Governance'
Recording 'for training purposes'
The anxious tremor in your voice

How many bits of you are there?

And this vetting procedure
That harbours our darkest desires,
Its wavering attention,
Its careful perplexity—

Believe in it. What else is there?

And another justice secretary's
'Non-conviction disposals',
Each one a licence then
To break into your past

It's what we'll find, one day, in your saliva

And you? You sit here, wondering
How far your art can take you
Until you'll disappear like that young man
And later you'll emerge, as something perfect?

The citizen unharmed

Invisible harm! As if
Each one of us were waiting to be rescued.
Taking a picture of the sky?
But there's too much sky for a photograph.

Forbidden

And here it comes, the high gaze down at you
From under a peaked cap
Or else a disk containing most of you
A piece of plastic pressed against the flesh

Scaly like a politician's handshake

Thick animal smell, the burden that is 'you'.
Meanwhile you thought it was a private art
Since armed in secret
There is the distance your art gives you

However much it dances . . .

four: the baffler

A usually static device that regulates the flow of a fluid or light. A partition that prevents interference between sound waves in a loudspeaker.

Whose mouth split like a reed
might turn towards me
the direction of the satisfied air

Vantage Point

I arrived at Gagliano one afternoon in August, ha
ndcuffed, in a small unsteady car. My hands were
handcuffed and I was accompanied by two large
representatives of the stat, strong from the red stripes
on their trousers to the expressionless looks on their
faces. I was coming not of my own free will, prepard
to encounter any form of ugliness,   because I had been
ordered, by   been forced, by an unexpected order, to
leave Grassano where I had lived previously and where
I had got to know Lucania.   G., like all the little
town round here, is a white affair on the top of a high
abandonded mountain range, like a miniature Jerusalem
imaginary in the solitude of the dese t. I loved to
climb the summit to the town, up to the wind-battered
church, from where the eye could look out on every
direction on a limitless horizon, identical in every
stretch of the circle. It is liie the middle of a sea
of - land, monotonous and treeleass: the towns white and
distant, each one glued to its hillside, . .. the lands
and cavern of brigands, right down to where perhaps lies
the sea,.. I felt as if I had guess ed the obscure value
of this blasted land, and that I had begun to love it:
it bothered me to be moving.…

> Fluttering to the floor,
> Like all the others a white hilltop affair,
> Monotonous, treeless, towns white and distant,
> An abandoned mountain, the consolation of exile.
> It bothered me to be leaving
> Its limitless horizon
> Identical in every stretch of its circle,
> A thing of obscure value

*The piece of typescript that fell out of the second-hand book I'd just bought
was evidently someone's draft translation—a piece of homework perhaps—
of a passage from Carlo Levi's* Christ Stopped At Eboli, *where the author
describes his exile as a political prisoner of the Italian Fascist government.*

Began

What I began began me.
The words seemed startled to inherit
What was I, as if stepping
Cautiously into the sun was a boy
Who almost knew how to be happy.

Leaving the beach, gathering children and towels
A steepness of evening sunlight
Lay on house-fronts. Here was where
The good-enough mother might finally
Encounter the good-enough child?

Do I remember it,
That being reflected back?
Being welcomed into the mirror
Difference there met likeness
The eyes kept careful as distance.

Now, looking into a room
Prepared as if for absence
Light crinkling in the lampshade,
While outside like a change of weather
Is the 'life that waits for no one'

The sky walks away on its hands.
But it may be you are still working in there
In silence stretching the paint,
Bridging a certain absence, brought into play
Like the gap between two clouds

As I lower myself uneasily into the picture.

Braque: Atelier
Or Why Does Watching Birds Make Me Happy?

Watching her staple the canvas to its stretcher then coat it with rabbit-glue size. Drying, it extends across the floor—it's like an enormous bird-trap. Later there are the sounds I hear her making in there as I walk past the door. When she cranks the easel up and down it sounds like the sewing machine, or there's a scuffling sound of brush-strokes like a rabbit scraping the ground. Then silence. I peer round the door. Outside the window I catch sight of a pigeon's strong-shouldered flight, and there she is stretched out on the sofa asleep. Watching her feels like watching the sunshine on the wall outside.

'Obsessively related to the soul'
A star-shaped embryonic bird.
He'd perched it in his mind,

This one, who sits like a priest with his shapes
Believing in nothing—
'This is what I prepare'.

…

'They were born on the canvas'
Or so he said.

The bird approaching,
It's a shape torn out of paper

Its flight paint's weight on canvas,
The wet substance. Slowly it dries.

In full flight, imagined it
Crashing into a large black cloud

Its flight consuming the air. Down here
Can colour weigh as much

Where the studios are spread out everywhere
Like enormous bird-traps?

...

How can this sturdy bundle
Of blood bones and nerves

So steady itself in the air
To stay upright?

The paintings are all below you now
They live like this hidden inside their houses

And there's something inside a word
Like an outbreak of light.

Caught in an angle of light, the wing
Is a shape that traverses a canvas blind,

Its alien, stiff feel –
Look how it's leaving your hand

For that laziness in the air! Now, wonder
How it is they can ever return

Who did their best to rise
Towards what they can never find.

A studio's full of dead things
But this one, it saves itself in the air,

A bird trapped in the act of returning
To a nest shaped like a hand

Instructed in the art of it,
A revised form of madness

Who took the life that was in it,
Consumed it feathers and all!

But still the image was of flight
Steadily towards morning,

That sense of self,
Hugging it close, it was like the remains of a dream

And with this beak it opened its desire

Heron

And this heron, he is no angel
In his cloak of wings—coming down
To the pond in my garden each morning
He invites himself to breakfast.
But those are *my* frogs
Though I must admit I feel privileged sometimes
At his lofty arrival here
Whom hunger guides each morning
But surely too large for my small garden.
He is always in sight of death
Lifting high each careful unwebbed foot.
I notice—I cannot help it—how
It's all to one purpose, this killing machine
With its concentrations of stillness.
Thoughtful he seems, thought-heron
Who is everything brought to a point.
He is a finished thing
While, being here busy with language,
I feel like the old man I saw in the street
Both hands on his stick and entirely
Preoccupied with his walking.

I open the door, heron turns
To look at me for a moment—
What is it he recognises
Before going back to his island
In the reservoir? It's a mile or so from here

Where he nests untidily in the trees
And the frog he lets fall when I startle him –
The mangy fox, brush gone to a piece of string,
Arriving later will hold it
Sideways in his jaw, twisting and snapping.

But heron—just watching one,
It can start to make you feel good
Before he unhurriedly lifts and floating away
Goes into a fold in the air,
A substanceless sign. So how did he learn
To be so alone in the sky?
As upwards he sails, breasting my thought
The play of him will continue
In here to enlarge my mind
As if I imagined mornings
When he and I might breakfast together.

Untitled Talk

The ends of my body, its breath.
Lying here I'm chasing odd phrases.

It had become a trick
this making yourself significant
ie that you
signify, you
stand for something

and yr dislocated prose   the breath of life?
It's a sort of inward diary.
Here I am in its odd renewal.
There's that certain set of the words
while the voice that inhabits me,
it's the words, at a certain angle.
Do they know it   and if so how can they tell?

A transparency, holding it off
being held safe,
where the summer rain brings a heave
of vegetation right up to the window
quite close to the glass.
It might be such a relief
inside here, the slightness of us.

It is just a small mouthful
to be cradled in my smell—
it was there   just before the page dried
that we all fell asleep, in our poses

The Thief of Light

The wife of the pioneer Victorian photographer
Fox-Talbot referred to his camera as 'the mousetrap'.

Where the land gets to the sea
There are trees, as if in a painting
And berries you can't identify
But you feel ought to be of some use.
A church clock striking marks the occasion.
It beckons you to silence
And as if you see what sees you
A 'mousetrap', the thief of light
Starts blinking, having about it
Already that flavour of possession.
It is always pointing things out
In order to take them away.
Crossing the estuary now you can see
Two figures in the far distance
As if they were moving out of a painting.
Holding and losing balance here
Are equally mysterious.
You carry on up to the cliff top, stretch out
At the edge. Straw-coloured grass stems
Are arranged like notes of music
Between you and the ocean.
From somewhere far behind you
The artist is shouting for help
While those two are still hesitating
In their land-and-water world.

The Granite Bowl in the Berlin Lustgarten, by Hummel

"It was decided that a particularly large bowl should adorn Berlin itself, and work began on an eighty ton granite block that took two years to grind and polish..." The painting, by Hummel, who was a Professor of Optics, shows a small crowd of people gathered round the bowl gazing up at their reflections on its underside.

People reflected upside-down
In the bowl's underside, being
Drawn like us to its unrelenting surface
Seem oddly apart from themselves.
They are finding in this abrupt light
A blankness of appearance
Made manifest. The bowl itself
Is like an upturned all-reflecting eye
And even the patient shapes of cloud
Seem suddenly rushing up
Towards its alluring strangeness
While the people in the painting have
A slightly stunted look, like
Figures from a fairy tale.
Voluptuaries of emptiness
They observe their twisted reflections
Or else look out at you
As if fallen silent at the site of some
Tremendous accident
And slowly they will now
Begin, like us, to circumambulate
An enormous pointlessness.

At Hunstanton

for Peter and Lynn
'increasingly breathtaking views'
Peter Hughes

1. Hunstanton Cliff Event

Cliff recession rates
Cliff behaviour model
Cliff failure information: detailed analyses
Both temporal and spatial prediction
At critical structure locations

Cliff behaviour zone
Individual failure events
Failure mechanisms involved
In cliff regression
                  Mitigation measures

Where the land is shedding itself
The old lighthouse stays unsold.
On the beach you find scrolls of birch bark
Floated over from Norway
And lumps of peat that look like oil.
They are remains of a forest
Now drowned under sea. You dry them out
And burn them inside your stove.
Outside people are walking their dogs,
In a green interim
                  between houses and edge.

2. In The Sensory Garden, Boston Square, Hunstanton

Marsh Hawkshead
                    Rough Clover
Many-spiked Goosefoot
                          Seaside Catchfly—
They are names you can't quite believe in.
A couple of hundred yards inland
The plants' outlines are sculpted
Just underneath each name
On slabs, arranged in a semi-circle
Like irregular gravestones.
The names are in braille as well, raised dots
On small strips of metal glued down
And you think of a hand that brushes against
The almost-substance of words
Then turn and look down the slope.
In the middle-distance is some kind of fir tree
Leaning slightly. It looks like a character
As if it bowed to the water beyond it
And all the sea's names.

The Days

Twenty past six am. Tinnitus
Is the noise in my right ear,

The hairs in my ear's inner chamber
That bend and wave to a breeze of sound.

When I wake abruptly as if I am drowning in air
I practice breathing to stop this insistent sound,

Getting up   leaving the bedroom—
My body, its self-imaginings,

Is walking towards me out of the mirror.
Incontinent it keeps on writing things down.

It's a rhythm I've picked up somewhere
Persistent as the noise in my ear.

The clean living smell—
It's the sense of her in the mind

And petals underfoot, so much
Crushed detail

It makes a sort of reverse pilgrimage
Where the pear-blossom gets walked inside the house.

Outside on the grass and densely scattered
It dazzles

As if what the words conceal
Is what I am always moving towards

And I'll try to disturb the surface of things
As little as possible.

Jardin des Plantes

The iceland poppies are on the march
bright white day
all the things we ought to look at—
thinking is a space to fill with words.
In the name of the human
vigilance propreté
animals are being torn apart
all along one side of the museum
while all the men of science, a row of heads
stare sternly out.
Yes evolution is murder!

Along the river bridges wrapped in silence
and sculpture   on this one's backside
someone has written NINA.
Madame defend me from
your inconsequential observations
I believe everything I can say
imagining life on that balcony over there
painted with sunlight like an impressionist picture.

Musée de l'art moderne: graffiti
A building wears the art on its sleeve . . .

A machine for thinking us with
one perfect spring morning.
Here or hereabout
there was something called I
whose feet in small steps covered the city

and these 'poems'
  versions made
    at a great distance

but sudden all the same
  & browsing among the rubbish—I
    look up—an abrupt museum

  as if the windows took flight
    dinosaur skeletons glimpsed
      through windows set high in the wall

                    Paris, April 2010

Tate (Modern)

1
'It formed a sort of trail
the energy of the magnetic fields
continues to orient the needle
it is kept alive'.

Where 'north' spreads its skirts, rivers and mountains
'waves of slowly solidifying foam'
'divided astral mess'
it's almost an exact copy!

copying angels—
they fled apart
the spirit of the empty
art like a stain on the gallery wall?

a stepladder   up to the sky
'two booths, dispensing kites and umbrellas'

'actions and interventions
that take place in landscape'
Is enough being said?

'The hanging wool teased out to mimic paint'

2

Where a blameless sun expired in the mind of the gallerist
A new procession's arriving. Where the gallerist
Expired there's a stain on the pavement.
They were taking him home by the sleeve
And his explanations? That was the fine grey dust
His notices were intended to dispel,
What otherwise might thicken like an abrupt soup.
Something diffuse and ancient's behind us now
And, once they broke open the tomb,
It was music to quieten the century.
But here at the top of the building
We're drawing what we can *see*. Look down—
It's that moment we all wave our programmes in the air
Till, blinded with the obvious, it's time to go home.

Breeze's Counsel

They forget the dust for a little music
                                        Roland Penrose

Glad to be there
                        Not any longer, for now
This interval, of
                        walking
Back to it, over the leaves—
A breeze blows the shadows about
As if we were inside it
Like a slightly disordered mind.

What language blinks at
As light as hunger
Gets covered with a cloth of sound

Like watching birds it's always
Just over there the
Startled life in it,

Some significant birdsong
And I only write it down, to defend myself
From all that noise.

Given almost enough with which to dissemble
The words like someone shamming dead
Whose inscriptions battle the stillness
Or like the names of stations rushing past
Each one is a petrified blessing.
Till calmed by snow the silent other
Is lifted onto the arms of trees
White perfume cooled to zero.

What might be spilt becomes an effect of silence,
The future sealed for a time
And later, to see it slipping away,
A tainted patchwork effect,
The unheard sound as epitaph.

The brush-and-ink poets
Are tracing their names.

Halting lyric a nagging wish:
'He Carries His Instrument Home'.

What I dismember,
Yes take it home, splash it with wine

In a city whose poor are pushed to its rim.
Cheap orchids   breeze's counsel

Ash Cloud, Kew Gardens

And somewhere like a window swinging open
                                    somewhere
A landscape with its mouthings of trees.
There are the words that will not need you
Collecting in silence all around your mouth.
They make it sound as if you almost meant it
And you want to settle the words inside you,
This language lining a mouth,
A careful heap of fallen petals. All the same
Distracted from 'self', set free to rhapsodize
You think it really ought to last for ever.

Lifting the camera, as if it were
A sort of prayer.
But the language was an accident
That happened somewhere in the creature's brain.
Can you afford the planet?

A jay can bury five thousand acorns in autumn.
Somewhere inside this amiable jungle
There waits a label not designed to be read.
Here at the edge of what we almost know
It flowers, as if in hiding.
Together we have come
To the edge of what we were saying
Hung out in rows, like changeless blossom
Against a sky whose blue
Once made us intensely happy.
But noticed most when gone,
Our words like scented gardens for the blind.

Whose Breaths

. . . and our words turn and fall
flickering with our life upon the earth.
                              Andrew Crozier

The last Rastafarian, a lonely tribal singer.
There are women with armfuls of children.
The god is a floating cargo.

The burden was somewhere in front of me,
Shone, lazily. Stepping out
Into a hidden romance of storms

The absence that there is in me
Was what I found to celebrate,
A fresh quiet smell. Shallow epiphany

To have found it again intact,
The thoughtful container,
Its shifting stain of consciousness.

On the lip of its
Creatureliness, to live
Without consolation?

The poem ending it happens again and again
Like hearing from far off the sound of land,
Speech acts the saviour

As if we imagined returning
The things to their proper names,
The plainness of our speech being fed to earth.

Its Halting Measure

I go down at daybreak to see.
Something is being dismembered
Out there under the trees?
There's that quality of first light, its
Silent estrangement,
And the deep parental silence,
Their dense sleep overhead.
This kitchen—its lack of amenities pleases
As it might be the nineteen fifties
I think there are more rooms here
Half-used, waiting to be discovered.
Beside me now the cat's all attention.
There's something familiar about this animal
Her back arched under my hand.
I too perhaps am made for one thing,
Such an absolute attention
As I go on watching and being watched—
Is there something out there that might complete me,
Something that's there for the taking?
But for now this austere daybreak.
Those two upstairs, they have gone now
Who were clearing a space for me with their lives.
They have taken away their blanket of breathing
And there comes, as if to inhabit me,
A voice stepping neatly out of its silence.
As if you might learn the trick of it, suddenly
To contain   all words
                    such as *speechless*
And soon I shall have to make my way outside
Finally to find
The satisfaction of its halting measures.

The Wind Harp

This thing, that's half out in the air
With a door for the breeze to enter
It is here, again
With its supper of winds.

Notes

The Voice in a Mirror The epigraph to this was seen on the side of a building, possibly a college of printing, while waiting for a bus in Heidelberg.

After de Tabley The quote is from the Victorian poet de Tabley's poem 'The Graveyard on the Sands'

Braque: Ateliers The poem refers to the bird motif that recurs in Braque's late paintings.

Alien Rhapsody The two lines in italics were notices in Kew Gardens, visited on the day in 2009 when the planes had been silenced by the ash cloud from the Iceland volcano. "They make you sound as if you almost meant it"—this was a mother reproving her child for the way he said goodbye when she was collecting him from a friend's birthday party: "That sounded a bit poetic. Make it sound as if you really meant it."

'In Riots Of the Upper Air' The London-based Iraqi poet Fawzi Karim's collection 'Plague Lands and other poems' appeared in English translation from Carcanet in 2011.